*M*AKING YOUR LIVING AS A
STRING
P L A Y E R

CAREER GUIDANCE FROM THE EXPERTS
AT *Strings* MAGAZINE

Edited by GREG CAHILL

Visit Hal Leonard Online at
www.halleonard.com

In Australia Contact:
Hal Leonard Australia Pty. Ltd.
22 Taunton Drive P.O. Box 5130
Cheltenham East, 3192 Victoria, Australia
Email: ausadmin@halleonard.com

STRING LETTER PUBLISHING

EXCLUSIVELY DISTRIBUTED BY

HAL•LEONARD® CORPORATION

7777 W. BLUEMOUND RD. P.O. BOX 13819 MILWAUKEE, WI 53213

AUG   2004

Contents

Introduction

Here are two true stories.

I played in a nursing home recently for an old, sickly gent in a wheelchair. After I finished, I put my hand on his knee and said, "I hope you get better real soon." He looked up at me, scowled and said, "I hope you get better real soon, too."

One time at a bluegrass gig I played the tune "Kentucky Waltz." Out of the corner of my eye, I saw an old man in the front row, crying. Afterwards I went up to him and said, "Sir, you must be from Kentucky." He said, "Nope. I'm a musician."

Congratulations. You've decided to become a professional string player. *Strings* magazine has published this helpful folio to help you navigate the treacherous shoals and challenging inlets of this bizarre and gratifying world of the professional string player.

Increasingly, contemporary string players have to be able to do it all. In my experience, I have played gigs ranging from the Renaissance group the Waverly Consort (very quiet) to rock 'n' rollers Jimmy Page and Robert Plant of Led Zeppelin (very loud). I've taught human beings from ages five to 95 (and learned a great deal from those people, too). I've played over a thousand weddings. At one, the band took a break and got in line at the buffet table. The maitre d' came over to me and angrily said, "You can't eat there. The people eat there."

Anyway, in this book you'll find helpful tips on preparing your resume, what to expect while doing weddings (the unexpected), how to handle holiday stress, the do's and don'ts of busking, setting up a teaching studio, gigging overseas, and much more. Whatever you choose to do (and you'll probably end up doing all of it), you can rest assured that you'll be happy, because playing a string instrument is a blast. A total blast.

And those two stories at the beginning? Well, they didn't happen to me, but something just as memorable will happen to you. When it does, please let me know about it!

—*Matt Glaser*

Matt Glaser is chairman of the String Department at the Berklee College of Music in Boston. He has published four books on contemporary violin styles including *Jazz Violin*, coauthored with the late Stephane Grappelli. Matt was an advisor for Ken Burns's PBS documentary "Jazz," and serves on the board of directors of Chamber Music America.

The growing importance of paperwork stems from the fact that, with budgets tightening and formerly secure ensembles fighting for survival, more than ever rides on the performance of each musician in an orchestra.

—Robert L. Doerschuk

Résumé Required

1

TIPS ON COMPILING YOUR PROFESSIONAL CREDENTIALS

By Robert L. Doerschuk

ONE OF THE MANY REASONS I decided to be a musician was to avoid having to schlep my *curriculum vitae* around in search of work. Well, guess what? Not only do I have to wear a suit and tie for most of my gigs, I'm also finding that résumés have become a fact of life in the music world.

The growing importance of paperwork stems from the fact that, with budgets tightening and formerly secure ensembles fighting for survival, more than ever rides on the performance of each musician in an orchestra. While common sense suggests that picking the best players is how you get the best people, there's actually a lot more involved in that selection than how someone sounds in an audition.

For example, a virtuoso violinist may be absolutely wrong for a seat in the violin section, or even as concertmaster, according to Donald Portnoy, music director of the Augusta (Georgia) and University of South Carolina Symphony Orchestras. "When I was studying at Juilliard I had some friends who were fantastic fiddle players," he explains. "But when I sat next to them in the orchestra, I could hear them getting lost all the time. They could play circles around people when they were doing Paganini, but that didn't mean they could look at an orchestra part and play it immediately. In today's world, because no one has the time or money to rehearse and rehearse, orchestra players have to do things very quickly."

These sorts of strengths aren't always apparent in auditions. Nor can they normally be made clear through word of mouth; to avoid litigation over charges that one candidate got preferential treatment because of prior contact with the hiring committee, most orchestras severely limit access to information about applicants at auditions. More than ever, these take place now behind closed doors—or, literally, behind screens that block the committee's view of the performer during blind auditions. Carpets are often laid down behind the screen as well, to muffle the telltale click of high-heels, the tread of army boots, or any other gender giveaways.

Where to Begin

Under these restrictive conditions, it becomes your responsibility to supplement your audition with a persuasive résumé.

While it's easy to put one together that actually operates against your better interests, it's even easier to score points just by following a few simple rules.

Most important, be concise; never submit a résumé that runs longer than one page. Use high-quality paper, with strong contrast between the type and the background, since many personnel directors will read about you in the dim light of the auditorium as you're playing onstage. Although some orchestras now invite prospective members to submit résumés by email, it's still best to snail mail yours in, so that you retain control over its appearance.

As to the content, that will vary somewhat, depending on your history and the proclivities of the committee. Seasoned players might want to display their professional experience at the top of the sheet, tailored to the needs of the position they're hoping to fill. If, for example, you're vying for a chair in the middle of the violin section, it would make sense to emphasize your track record of playing in similar positions, even if that means downplaying whatever appearances you've made as a soloist or in smaller groups. On the other hand, recitals would count for more when a first-chair or concertmaster opportunity presents itself.

No matter where you list your credits, arrange them in reverse chronological order. "The most recent work should always come first," says Tom Hadley, personnel manager at the Baltimore Symphony Orchestra. "I get a lot of résumés where the latest performances, which are often also the most interesting, are buried deep in the text. If I'm not careful, I might wind up missing it."

Players with a shorter track record should focus instead on their training. Derek Mithaug reached this conclusion after teaching classes in résumé writing at the Juilliard School, where he serves as director of the career development office. "We have an exercise," he says. "We provide students with stacks of résumés, which they separate according to which ones they like and dislike. Over and over again, we've found that education, at least from their perspective, was a key criterion. If you're coming from a name school that specializes in preparing young musicians to be performers, then it would be very advisable to put education as perhaps your first category."

Donald Portnoy agrees. "Let's be very honest: when somebody sends you a résumé that says Curtis Institute or Juilliard, you're going to say, 'Hmm, I want to listen to this.' And when you get a résumé from somebody in South Dakota, even if that person might play better than someone from Curtis, you're less likely to hear them out."

If your credentials aren't as stellar as your playing, you may be tempted to look for some way to make your presentation stand out. If so, *don't do it*. You may be the funniest viola player in town, but any attempt to go beyond the bare facts will backfire. Greg Olson, the principal bassist and personnel manager at the Owensboro (Kentucky) Symphony Orchestra, points out that he and his colleagues read résumés as they're listening to auditions; if anything on the page proves distracting, the inclination is to move along to the next candidate.

Too much information can be just as counterproductive. Aside from your name, instrument, and contact information, followed by education and performance credits in whichever order is appropriate, anything else is probably superfluous. References, for example, are generally considered unnecessary at the résumé stage, unless you're applying for a principal position.

"And even then," Olson says, "they should be listed at the bottom of the page."

Supplemental Materials

Opinions are mixed over whether to submit a recording with your résumé. At Owensboro and other community orchestras, they're not required, since almost everyone applying for a position is allowed a live audition. Larger ensembles may find them useful, however, in winnowing out the strongest from a large field of candidates. It's best to check with the orchestra's business office before making your decision.

Photos, on the other hand, are never advisable—for one thing, they obviously violate the idea of blind auditions. Ditto for bios, even if you can compress your personal history down to one paragraph. "Bios can be misleading," says Charles Letourneau, president of Impresario Arts, a consulting firm for classical musicians. "When I see a bio, I get the feeling that someone is trying to spin something."

In the end, your résumé can make the difference in getting the gig. Portnoy remembers a résumé that was especially well prepared that influenced him to hire one applicant for a position over another that he actually knew better. "They were very close to each other, but we took the one we didn't know because that person spelled out their relevant experience more clearly."

It comes down to this: there are more talented musicians than ever in search of work. "It's partly our fault, because we keep producing them," Portnoy laughs. But you and you alone are in charge of putting your résumé together; to that degree, at least, your future can depend on how persuasively you spell out your past on paper.

When musicians agree to come out of their practice rooms and play for pay in front of others, the arrangements and expectations need to be precise.
                                        —Tom Heimberg

The Paper Chase

2

CONTRACT TIPS FOR THE GIGGING PLAYER

By Tom Heimberg

"Dear Mr. Heifitz, please come to my birthday party. (P.S. Don't forget to bring your violin.)"

THERE IS MUSIC FOR ALMOST EVERY KIND of human gathering, and musicians are often asked to play it—for free. Through the learning years, as a player's skill grows, the number of requests to play at special events grows, too. Students are asked to play in school and in church; schoolmates are asked to play at dances; friends are asked to play at weddings.

It is natural and healthy for musicians to spread goodwill while gaining experience and reputation. But there comes a moment (different for everyone) when the process turns professional. Money is offered—or asked for—and then new dimensions of mutual obligation are established between musicians and their listeners.

When that starts to happen, both sides are best served by making clear agreements about the forthcoming exchange. How much music is expected? How much money will be paid? What else do both parties need to know? When musicians agree to come out of their practice rooms and play for pay in front of others, the arrangements and expectations need to be precise. And they need to be written down. That way there is less chance of anyone being disappointed.

Making agreements—and sticking to them—is one of the most important human activities. I have heard many people express annoyance and impatience with written agreements: "Why be so formal?" "Can't people trust one another?" "Can't business be done honorably with a simple handshake?" Anyone who can shake hands with honor can sign with honor. Agreements should be written because the human mind is complex and human memory is fallible. (Have you ever misplaced your keys? Mixed up appointments you hadn't written down?)

The other reason to commit the agreement to writing is that the different parties involved can come to different conclusions at the end of a conversation, without even realizing it. I was once present at the end of a business discussion between a friend and his mother. It went like this: "Well, that sounds pretty good, Mom. Let's write it up." "Oh no, dear. We don't have to write anything. I'm your mother; I trust you." "Mom, don't trust me! We've been talking for an hour and a half. We've discussed all kinds of possibilities. How do we know that when we leave this room we'll both remember the same things? We have to write something; it's the only way we can be sure that we agree."

That's one of the most compelling arguments in favor of memoranda that I've ever heard. Not to mention that they help fend off the legal worries implied by film producer Samuel Goldwyn's famous quote, "A verbal agreement isn't worth the paper it's written on."

Although the process of reaching an agreement is sometimes complicated, writing a memo of that agreement should be kept simple. You don't need anything more complicated than a blank sheet of paper. The clearest format is the following modification of an old newspaper formula. Start with the *date* and *time*, and then list this sequence:

Who: Who is making the agreement? Who will be playing? Who will be paying?

What: What will be played, and how much of it? Are there any special requests to be honored, or any special prohibitions to be respected?

Where: The location of the event, and whether it is an indoor or outdoor setting.

When: The time of the event, including advance time for setting up, the number and lengths of breaks, and the ending time.

How much: Agree on the pay, and on how and when it will be provided. Will it be in installments? Do you need an advance of good-faith money?

Once those important parameters have been established, go on to more specific details. If you or your group have special needs, this is the opportunity to list them. Help non-musicians know what is important to you—for example, lighting requirements, chair requirements, protection from the elements if you are to play outdoors, etc. This is also the place to list the client's special requirements. Will the dress be formal or casual? Is there a wedding ceremony whose musical pattern has to be outlined and planned?

If all this is beginning to sound complicated, rest assured that it doesn't have to be. Details always add up; that's what they do. But they fall into broad categories that you can organize ahead of time. With experience, you will come to recognize concerns that show up over and over again. You can use the above formula as a template for generating your own personal checklist.

Stick to Your Word

Then you can go further. As your group works more and more, the agreement process can be aided by turning the checklist into a prepared form. A musician's earliest playing experiences are usually with friends and family, and in those relationships, complications can (ideally) be worked out smoothly as they occur. But as you start to deal with people you know less well, remember that the more you can prepare ahead of time, the better off everyone will be. This is where a contract form can facilitate negotiations. The pictured sample shows how details can be organized into a helpful and businesslike contract. Keep it simple; one page is all you'll need (until you land touring and recording contracts).

If demand grows and you find yourself playing often, you should give serious consideration to joining the musicians' union. Speaking as a longtime member and former steward myself, I believe there are many benefits to joining, including the availability of standard contract forms and established pay scales. Negotiations are easier when there is a base to work from.

Now that you know how to write agreements, remember the next step: keeping them. Be dependable. Do everything you can to plan ahead, to be prepared, and to be punctual. The virtuoso who shows up at the wrong place or on the wrong day is still a virtuoso, but is not appreciated as much. And the contract has been broken.

Making—and writing—clear agreements is a simple but important act that improves the final musical experience. It helps everyone, employers and musicians alike. Once needs and expectations have been made clear, all the participants can go into the event with ease and confidence. Try it; everyone will like it.

Good luck with your projects—and with your music making.

Your String Quartet
Performance Agreement

YSQ contact :_____   Phone : _____

                                              Address : _____

                                              _____

Client name:_____

We will perform at your:_____

On: (date) _____Location:_____
(Please include a map or adequate directions to the site when the contract is returned.)

Starting time:_____   Ending time:_____
(We will arrive 15 minutes in advance of the starting time to set up.)

♦ Please indicate whether you prefer us to wear *formal* (black dresses for women, and tuxedoes for men) or *casual* dress (dresses/skirts for women, and suits for men).
Formal_____Casual_____

♦ We require four chairs **without** arms. If we are to play outdoors, we **must** be in an area which is protected from the wind and **completely** shaded from the sun.
Will this be an indoor_____ **OR** an outdoor_____ event?

Our first hour of performance will be without a break. We will take a 10-minute break for each additional hour of playing.

In addition to works on our repertoire list, we can play specific music by arrangement. We must, however, have **at least** 2 weeks notice for any special requests. Please list necessary information for wedding ceremonies on a separate sheet. Be sure to include where in the ceremony the music is to take place, and for whom (e.g. bridal processional; bridesmaids' processional; seating of mothers; bridal recessional, etc.).

The total charge for your event is $_____. In order to reserve the date of performance, we must receive a 50% (non-refundable) deposit on this charge. The remaining balance is due at the completion of our performance. **Please make checks payable to the contact person listed above.**

Feel free to call us if you have any questions or wish to make further arrangements.

YSQ contact signature : _____   Date :_____

♦ *I have read and approved the above and am including a 50% deposit of $ _____
with the return of this agreement.*

(Please sign and date)   _____

Freelancing can be a liberating way of making a living as a string player. Every job is an adventure, and the variety can be incredibly stimulating.

—Jana Luckey

Building a Freelance Career

3

FOR THE MOTIVATED PLAYER, CREATING YOUR OWN NICHE CAN LEAD TO A LUCRATIVE LIVING

By Jana Luckey

FREELANCING CAN BE A TERRIFIC WAY to make a living as a musician. Career freelancers are some of the best sight readers around, they are expert at playing different styles of music, and they can be as adaptable and flexible as the best opera musicians. But establishing yourself as a freelancer can be a challenge. What steps can you take to get the desirable work in town—whether it's playing Broadway shows, performing in the pit for the local ballet, playing with a symphony, or even gigging with a good quartet—and how can you find enough of this work to support yourself?

Make Contacts

Building a freelance career begins with making contacts—lots of them. You'll have a leg up if you grew up or went to school in the area in which you want to work, because you'll already know people and be familiar with the local performing-arts scene. If, instead, you're moving to a new city and hoping to freelance, do your homework. Go to the library and take a look at *Musical America*, a directory that lists thousands of performing-arts organizations state by state. Be sure to check out the listings for neighboring states, too: Indiana and

Michigan, for example, if you live in Ohio, or Connecticut and New Jersey if you live in downstate New York. After all, if you want to be a freelancer, you will probably have to do a fair bit of driving. Make sure you have a reliable vehicle to do it in!

After you've taken inventory of all the contacts you have in the area, you can begin the process of soliciting work. Call your friends and colleagues, and contact personnel managers and contractors by sending a résumé with a cover letter inquiring about playing opportunities. Make sure your résumé is typed, looks professional, and is completely up to date. Remember: until a potential employer gets to know your playing, your résumé is your calling card. It represents who you are and what you do, and it has to look good.

Get on Sub Lists

Orchestras and opera companies vary as to how they hire permanent players, extra players, and substitutes. While there is a national audition process for the permanent chairs in major symphonies, sometimes finalists or even semifinalists at these auditions are automatically added to the sub list. Some major orchestras hold local auditions on an as-needed basis to freshen up their pool of substitutes and extras. In this case, sending a résumé to the personnel manager should put you on the mailing list for notification of the next audition.

Sometimes it pays to take a more personal approach to getting on a sub list. Contact the principal player of your instrument's section—either with a résumé followed up by a phone call, or directly with a professional phone inquiry—and request to schedule a coaching. If the person agrees to hear you, prepare some typical audition repertoire, probably a concerto movement and a selection of orchestral excerpts. Look upon the experience as more of an audition than a lesson (although you should listen carefully to any advice given); present yourself well and don't be too coy about your intentions. If the principal player likes your playing, he or she may be forthcoming about subbing opportunities as well as upcoming local or national auditions.

Join Smaller Orchestras

Don't ignore the smaller and semiprofessional orchestras in the area. Especially if you're just out of school, an orchestra with a short season that performs the major repertoire can be an excellent place both to gain experience and to make contacts for other work in the area. Some of the most active wedding quartets come out of these orchestras, since full-time symphony players are often too busy to play such jobs. Your colleagues in these groups should have a good handle on other freelance activity in the area.

Join the Musicians' Union

As you explore all of these opportunities, don't forget that the musicians' union can be an important resource. If you are already a member of the American Federation of Musicians, join the local of the area where you plan to work. If you're not yet a member, you may have to join the local once you start accepting work from organizations with collective bargaining agreements. Membership in the union makes you part of a national network of musicians and also qualifies you for benefits such as the pension fund and certain types of insurance. The AFM Web site, at www.afm.org, has a searchable database of its locals, with contact information for each one.

The local itself may even provide a source of more work, since the office will know which contractors in town specialize in hiring string players. Some locals even hold an annual showcase where members can audition for contractors. In addition, many AFM locals have a referral service. If you're in a quartet that wants to play weddings and parties, or if you're a strolling violinist, be sure to register.

Set Up a Teaching Studio

If you enjoy teaching, setting up a studio is a great way to ensure a steady source of income. There are many ways to recruit students. You can contact the instrumental music teachers at the public schools and tell them of your availability. Community music schools in the area may have part-time teaching positions available. Make up a flyer advertising your services to post on bulletin boards in music stores, string shops, and music schools. Also, if you've attended school in the area or do some work with a local symphony, see if that school or orchestra will give your name out to callers seeking a string teacher.

Be Responsive

Once the phone starts ringing and those freelance jobs begin to roll in, there are a few things to remember about dealing with your new employers. Make sure that you have either a reliable answering machine or voicemail and that your message clearly identifies who you are in a professional manner. Check your messages frequently. A reputable contractor will call prospects one at a time, but he or she is only going to wait so long for a response before moving on to the next person on the list. Unless the contractor tells you differently, assume you have no more than 24 hours to respond to the job offer. If you ever need to back out of an engagement you've committed to, call the contractor immediately. Having to find last-minute replacements makes contractors crazy; the longer you wait to make that call, the less chance you have of being hired again.

Get the Details

When you accept a job, write down all the details. Sometimes a contractor will mail you a confirmation, but much of the time, you will be responsible for knowing when and where you will be playing. Be clear on the concert dress and whether you need to bring a music stand (it's an excellent idea to keep a folding stand in your car for emergencies). Find out what the repertoire will be and whether you will receive music in advance. If you are sent the music, consider making a personal copy or purchasing your own part for standard repertoire you may see again.

Be Professional

At the job itself, just do the basics. Arrive early to set up, tune, and look over the music. Be unfailingly friendly to everyone you meet. Watch the conductor (if there is one) like a hawk. Play your best, and remember to thank the contractor for hiring you. Contractors are creatures of habit, and they will generally hire their friends and the players they believe are most likely to be available. But if you approach every job with a terrific attitude and back it up with great playing, you will likely have a shot at getting that next call.

In the case of chamber-music jobs, very often you'll be dealing with people who aren't accustomed to hiring musicians and who will panic if you wander into the church five minutes before the "Wedding March." While playing a wedding may seem like just another gig to you—perhaps one of two or three ceremonies your quartet is playing that afternoon—respect the fact that the bride and groom consider it to be the most important day in their lives. Be professional in your dealings with the families, and look your best. After all, with the proliferation of wedding videos, you wouldn't want to be immortalized on tape in your wrinkled skirt or '70s-era bow tie.

Keep Records

No matter what kind of freelance work you end up doing, keep records. Develop a system to track mileage to and from jobs, any travel or meal expenses you incur at a job, and how much and when you are being paid. Especially if you are not paid on the day of the gig, it's very important when dealing with multiple employers to make a note of who owes you money and how much. (A significant advantage of doing work under an AFM contract is that you have recourse in case you or your group is stiffed.) Keep track of other expenses related to your freelance work, including such things as clothing you wear only for performances, strings and other musical supplies, and repairs to your instrument. These expenses may all be tax-deductible on Schedule C (Profit or Loss from Business) of the federal 1040 form that you will probably file as a freelancer.

Freelancing can be a liberating way of making a living as a string player. Every job is an adventure, and the variety can be incredibly stimulating.

Spending three hours reading through quartets at a reception or adapting to the style of a different conductor can be an exhilarating means of making good money. If you have a positive attitude, a professional demeanor, good organizational skills, and can really play your instrument, you should definitely give freelancing a try.

Despite the inroads of DJs, weddings offer string players a real opportunity to earn significant money or, in my case, build a career.

—Van Vinikow

Weddings? Just Say, 'I Do!'

4

IT'S NOT HARD TO BOOK DATES AND EARN GOOD MONEY— BUT START PLANNING NOW

By Van Vinikow

I HAVE THE BEST JOB IN THE WORLD. Every weekend from mid-May to late October my string quartet travels 45 miles west and several thousand feet up from Reno, Nevada, to majestic Lake Tahoe. There we play music for a carousel of couples who stammer, stutter, laugh, and cry through their marriage vows. With its fragrant pine forests, crystalline waters, and spectacular sunsets, Lake Tahoe is one of the most popular wedding destinations in the nation. My quartet visits lakeside mansions, enjoys outstanding food and drink, plays chamber and popular music (without tedious rehearsals), and gets paid in heartfelt compliments and bankable dollars.

But my job also involves sheep-dogging two dozen string players in six different trios and quartets. Like postal workers, we brave the elements: wind (the worst), rain (your bow hair will swoon), and even snow (fingers, what fingers?). I've discovered that a college degree does not necessarily signify common sense. Forgetting a music stand is one thing, but showing up without a bow? It happens.

I didn't set out to be a professional wedding musician. After college, my first destination was Reno and the exciting world of show business—just as nightclub employment began to decline. In 1982, a call to play at a wedding brought me to my senses: Every Saturday there's a wedding somewhere, and weddings need music. I wondered: Could a quartet that plays classical music for the ceremony, then popular music at the reception, drum up enough work to live on? The answer surprised me. Despite the inroads of DJs, weddings offer string players a real opportunity to earn significant money or, in my case, build a career. If you'd like to try your fingers at it, here are some important things you need to know.

Make Thee a Wedding Book

You'll need to play requests, and the traditional wedding songs—Wagner's processional, Mendelssohn's recessional—are not the most popular. (You'll learn to love a certain well-known "Canon in D.") If you plan on playing just the ceremony, you should be ready with at least 45 minutes of music in a variety of styles. Many versatile collections are available. We begin the prelude music as guests arrive, usually 20 to 30 minutes before the ceremony. Our starting selections are always in a major key

and not too slow. Since a third of our weddings include a singer, we arrange a rehearsal at least 45 minutes before the ceremony so the song will be fresh in everyone's minds.

Demand Professionalism from Your Colleagues

Playing outdoors can be a challenge. You need good-natured, reliable players in your ensemble, not complainers. At one April wedding, we played while huddled under a pine tree as snowflakes drifted down. The couple thought it so romantic that they rewarded us with a big tip. Keep that in mind.

Don't Forget to Market Yourself

Finding couples who are getting married isn't difficult—but it does take time and money. The promo package you send the bride is extremely important, since you won't get a second chance to make that first impression. If you're serious about grabbing a portion of the wedding pie, hire a designer to provide an original logo, envelopes, letterhead, and business cards. And pay a studio with a professional engineer to produce a top-notch demo, preferably a CD. I group 20- to 30-second excerpts of music into categories labeled "Prelude Suggestions," "Wedding Marches," "Recessional Choices," and so on. Make sure you spell all the pieces' names correctly, a little step that will save you time when the bride calls in a panic because the wedding program is "going to the printer tomorrow." It may also be worth placing a well-designed ad in your newspaper's wedding section, but be careful. I've found that attending a wedding fair brings more jobs than buying a small monthly ad in a newsprint handout. And don't forget that you can barter. My local symphony and opera offer ad space in their programs to musicians who'll play for performances. The beauty of this business is that the more weddings you play, the less you'll need to market yourself.

Keep a Grip on the Money

"True art is in the deal," Marcel Proust said, and the wise musician heeds his words. What should you charge? An hourly rate is standard, and your fee should include travel expenses. Ask some other groups what they get, if you can, and don't sell yourself short. I've always maintained that string musicians are worth more than others. My best advice? Start out reasonably, build a reputation, then slowly raise your prices.

Once you've set your fee, don't neglect to send an agreement or contract—getting the details in writing protects everyone. Include the date, time, location, group size (trio vs. quartet), fee per hour, and overtime. (You may want to specify that you'll be served a meal if you play for more than three hours.) Print shops offer two-sheet carbons, which make it easy for the bride to return a signed copy. My policy is to ask to be paid at least a week in advance. Last year a couple left their checkbook at the hotel, promised they'd mail a check the next day, then took off on their honeymoon in Italy—for two months.

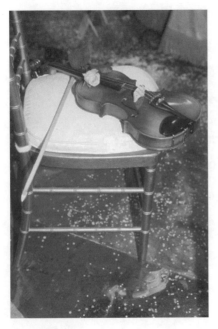

Plan Ahead

I once hired a feuding violist and cellist who refused to ride in the same car—and the cellist never found the gig. The aggrieved groom not only melted my phone after the wedding but demanded a refund, too. Experiences of that kind have taught me to carpool whenever possible.

As for dress, it doesn't matter what color you wear as long as it's black. For better or worse, customers expect formal wear; so, guys, I recommend shelling out for a comfortable and stylish tuxedo. Women, you'll have more leeway—in style, though not color. I also recommend a sturdy folding music stand, since you'll need the space when carpooling.

When you arrive you should know exactly what you will play for four key events: the seating of the mothers, the entrance of the bridesmaids, the bridal processional, and the bride-and-groom recessional. The seating of the mothers and grandparents traditionally launches the ceremony, so note this handy tip: when the photographer walks to the front of the hall, you know it's about to start. Music is often called for during the ceremony—the lighting of the unity candle, for instance, the rose presentation to the parents, or communion. My trick is to write everything on a ruled index card and clip it to my music. Since it can be hard to tell when to start and stop playing, position the group so the leader can see where the bride and bridesmaids enter and end up. I once had to count nine bridesmaids, three flower girls, and two ring-bearers from a church balcony while playing "Jesu, Joy of Man's Desiring," which, if you're unfamiliar with the sheet music for first violin, is one scrunched page of triplets. I was terrified to raise my eyes, knowing I would never find my place again.

FOOLPROOF MUSIC FOR WEDDING ENSEMBLES

My quartet tries to have a little something for everyone—classical favorites, show tunes, 1920s and '30s standards, country western hits, and a mix of ethnic melodies from Italian, Jewish, and Irish traditions. No single book will have everything you need, and to get the one song the bride really wants you can easily spend $30 or $40. That said, there are lots of options for building a wedding collection. Start with these trusty fake books:

The Wedding Album, compiled by Matthew Naughton, is filled with tasteful and legible arrangements. Call (415) 831-8058 or e-mail Naughton at mattmus@sirius.com.

The Wedding Album, Vols. 1 and 2, arranged by William Ryden (Masters Music Publication Inc. M1992, M2022), includes highlights such as the "Bridal Chorus" from Lohengrin and Schubert's Ave Maria.

Music for Three, Music for Four, and other volumes issued by Last Resort Music Publishing offer a wide variety of popular music. Review the volumes' contents at an easily navigable website: www.lastresortmusic.com.

continued...

Fortunately, the photographer was stuck in the balcony, too, and counted heads for me.

Of course, it's smart to chat up the officiant (minister, priest, rabbi) or wedding coordinator before the ceremony to review the order of events. If you're unsure when the vocalist will sing or when to start the communion music, just ask. Also find out exactly when the ceremony will end. At the kiss? The prayer? The introduction of the newly weds? (Tip: It's most often at the introduction.) Always play happy music for the recessional, and keep going until every guest has moved on.

Stay on Track During the Reception

If you know you'll be performing through lunch or dinner, try to position yourselves near where the bride and groom will sit, so they'll have a chance to hear you play. And keep it lively. I once worked a boisterous reception with a harpist who began with Bach's sluggish "Air on the G String." Guests won't always recall what you played, but they will remember the feel and tempo. Don't forget: You've been hired to help create a joyous mood, so stay away from slow movements of Mozart and the like. As the reception progresses, the chatter will grow louder, threatening to drown you out. Keep your chin up. Guests will appreciate you, even when they fail to applaud (they might spill their champagne).

We typically play an hour-long set, then break for ten minutes. It's easy to get distracted during your break by chatty guests and tasty hors d'oeuvres—so keep a sharp eye on your watch. If a meal is part of your deal, ask the caterers or servers to hold it

---

FOOLPROOF MUSIC FOR WEDDING ENSEMBLES

(continued)

Other Music Sources

The Hampton Quartet offers string arrangements of pop music by the Beatles, Led Zeppelin, and other rockers. To check out samples of their widely available sheet music, visit www.monalisasound.com.

For urgent needs, consider contacting a freelance arranger. Our group calls on a pop music resource known as The Lone Arranger (a.k.a. Steve Boone at (530) 541-5721).

for you until you're finished. Your players may complain, but it's not their signatures on your check.

Expect the Unexpected

Warn clients that if any part of the event takes place outside, you'll need shade to protect your instruments. Wind can likewise be a real problem. To secure your music in a breeze, buy some thin, springy hair clips (clothespins cover too much of the page). Accept that at some point you're certain to be set upon by an, er, loquacious guest with an emphatic request. If you can't honor it, offer something in a related style or by a similar composer, then start playing. Acknowledge compliments graciously, keep your business cards handy, and above all remember to smile. Perhaps the greatest reward of playing for weddings is knowing that you're sustaining the ancient tradition of live music on meaningful occasions. You get cake and champagne, too.

*We are hired to play well **and** to look good. Leave the grunge to the rockers— unless it's specifically requested.*

—Tom Heimberg

Be Prepared

5

HOLIDAY PLANNING
FOR THE BUSY MUSIC MAKER

By Tom Heimberg

THE CHRISTMAS, CHANUKAH, AND NEW YEAR holiday season can be the busiest time of the year for working musicians. In addition to the joys and efforts of shopping, gift-giving, and celebrating, an active string player might also fill the days—and nights—with the *Messiah*, the *Nutcracker*, and a New Year's Night in *Old Vienna.*

Along with this harvest of work and income can go hours and hours of driving, short nights of sleep, and meals eaten in a rush. In one familiar word: stress. Heavy scheduling intensifies the demands that professional musicians always face; demands that go beyond good musicianship. Playing well is just the beginning—to be successful, a musician has to be dependable. That means showing up at the right place, at the right time, on the right day, wearing the right clothes, holding the right instrument, being able to play the right notes at exactly the right moment—consistently, day after day. It means being organized and self-directed enough to meet all these requirements while still managing to stay rested, healthy, and positive.

These are high standards, but they can be met with the help of forethought and preparation, which smooths the way toward periods of intense work.

Through the years, my colleagues and I have found many useful devices for managing our busy musical lives. The following suggestions have been tested by experience. More significantly, they all derive from this important theme: when you plan ahead, you make things easier for yourself later.

Be Healthy and Rested

Taking good care of yourself always comes first. Good health and being in shape—both in your body and on your instrument—form the foundation for musical success. This is especially true when the workload is heavy. If you try to dive into a busy schedule after a break—a vacation, an illness, a life emergency—you risk soreness and injury.

You lessen that risk by coming to work with toned and practiced muscles. You further lessen it by warming up and cooling down effectively. Follow the principle "heat before playing, ice after playing." You can do this while you commute—a real time-saver. Even in temperate weather, consider wearing gloves while you drive. You can wear heat wraps on the way to the gig and cold packs on the way home, too.

All our lives we hear these bits of good advice: Practice, eat well, exercise, get enough sleep. Fine counsel, all of it. If we follow the advice conscientiously, we will find that each of these endeavors is a study in itself. I recommend the study, though I also recognize that this is not the place to prescribe a diet, or plan an exercise program. You will find your own. But there is one line of learning that deserves special mention: conscious relaxation—the intentional recognition and release of unnecessary tension in your body. Having an alert, calm mind in a healthy, relaxed body is a state of being. Entering this state sometimes requires special skill.

Relax

Good instrumental instruction should include training in techniques of self-scanning and tension release. The practice of these techniques should be part of daily life—relaxation and stress-reduction skills offer ever-increasing benefits when they are used through the years. Eliciting the relaxation response, using progressive relaxation or auto-genic training, or experimenting with 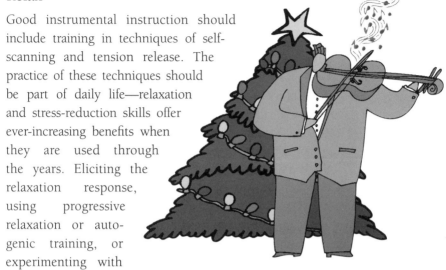 other exercises in mind/body relationship that often get lumped together under the word *meditation*—all those have a place in life and in music.

If you already know a technique that works for you, by all means keep using it. If you want to expand your knowledge, there are many avenues for doing so.

If you need a quick stress reliever, here's a simple one. I call it "the secret smile and the whispered 'ahh.'" First, sense the corners of your mouth and eyes. Then let go of any tension that you find there. Feel that you are smiling a secret smile. While you imagine this secret smile, whisper—or quietly sigh— "ahhh," as if you were trying to fog a mirror.

That's all there is to it. With these simple actions you have relaxed the two most immediate body responses to stress: a tensed face and tightened breathing. The subtle physical sensations are easeful and positive. Most people feel beneficial effects the first time they try this.

Care for Your Tools

Active players know the importance of a bow that still pulls sound, strings that hold their pitch, and an instrument that is free of mysterious buzzes and creaks. Take care of your instrument and it will take care of you. Is your instrument free of wolf tones or rattles? Are your strings fresh, and do you have a spare set in the case? Has your bow been rehaired recently? You can save yourself future worries by having your instrument adjusted well ahead of any period of intense work.

The same holds true for your car: a dependable set of wheels is extremely important for musicians on the move. Anyone who's going to do a lot of driving in December should have the car safety-checked in November. Good brakes, good tires, and a reliable battery and starter will eliminate many automotive worries and emergencies.

Once your car has been made safe, it can be outfitted to serve as Base Station during the coming weeks. Spare yourself those rushed last-minute searches: plan ahead, make a list of what you'll need, and provide it in advance: Do you wear glasses? Keep an extra pair in the car. Do you take medicines? Keep a spare supply there, too.

Have you been asked to bring your own stand to a job? Put two in the car trunk ahead of time—one for you and one for the colleague who forgot. Include stand lights and power cables, too, if you have them. I have not yet found battery-operated stand lights that are bright enough for me, but if they work for you, use them—and pack some back-up batteries as well. You *know* you're going to be asked to complete W-4, W-9, and I-9 forms; fill them out ahead of time and keep them in your car, or in your case.

You also know that you'll have to sit on often uncomfortable folding chairs, so keep a seat cushion and a back support in your car. They'll help make those long seated hours more livable. If it's not too much hassle for you to bring your own chair, do so. Take good care of yourself.

An Eye on Time

Another valuable tool is a good alarm clock. It can protect you from oversleeping and help you take short naps on busy days. Use a clock that can be set precisely, and that won't stop ringing until you turn it off. And if you've promised to do something at a specific time, write the promise on a Post-it note, stick it on the clock, and set the alarm.

Advance preparation can also extend to your cooking. If you prepare double meals now and freeze half for later, you'll thank yourself in the future. You also may want to outfit your car with a cooler, or even a small refrigerator that plugs into the cigarette lighter. You deserve a leisurely meal between services, but that's not always possible. And you might not want to depend on fast food. Sometime when you're trapped in traffic (it happens!) a handy, thoughtfully prepared snack or sandwich can make all the difference.

Dress for Success

Think ahead about your clothing, too. Adjust your performance dress for comfort and ease of playing. In our society, women musicians seem to have more leeway than men about the details of how they dress; they can find ways to be comfortable. Men have to finagle more, but there are things you can do. I wear lightweight, slightly oversized performance clothing, and I have had a pleat put in the back center seam of my jackets. Now there is no fabric tug when I raise my arms to play the viola. (Gussets under the arms can also have this effect.)

FOR FURTHER READING

The books of Dr. Herbert Benson are important resources for anyone interested in relaxation techniques. Read in sequence, they give an interesting view of the growth of his personal thinking along with his deepening research. *The Relaxation Response, Your Maximum Mind,* and *The Wellness Book* are all useful and relevant to our work. Visit www.mbmi.org/pages/bio1.asp for more information. *The Relaxation and Stress Reduction Workbook* by Martha Davis, Matthew McKay, Ph.D., and Elizabeth Robins Eshelman. (New Harbinger Publications, ISBN 1-879237-83-0) contains summaries of several of the techniques mentioned in this article.

Once your clothes are comfortable, they should also be clean and neat. We are hired to play well *and* to look good. Well-dressed, well-groomed musicians add to the festivity of the occasion. Leave the grunge to the rockers—unless it's specifically requested.

Practice thinking ahead and you'll find that early preparation always eases later stress. Anything helpful that you do ahead of time is a gift that you make to your future self. The gift will be appreciated, so be generous. It's in the holiday spirit.

I find it helps to be passionate about performing. Dance and sway to the music, enjoy yourself. Pour energy into the crowd, and it will generally be returned—both in smiles and tips.

—Heidi Montgomery

The Pavement Pays

6

TIPS ON STREET PERFORMANCE FOR PLEASURE AND PROFIT

By Heidi Montgomery

ASK ANY EXTREME-SPORT ENTHUSIAST the reason for hurtling headlong down steep and often snow-clad mountains, clinging finger and toe to stony precipices, and the response will undoubtedly have something to do with thrill and challenge, personal glory and achievement. Ask any musician, whether soloist or fourth-chair cellist, what makes him or her walk out on stage time and again and, vocabulary aside, the answer is essentially the same. Whether racing around boulders and trees or through a string of rapid-fire 16th notes, the heart can pound and the adrenaline pump. And both can be addictive.

As addictions go, the lure of performing is no great cause of distress, unless, of course, the addict has insufficient access to concert halls, coffeehouses, or bar gigs. The solution? Hit the pavement! Create your own venue and go where the people are. I'm talking about street performance or, as it is more commonly known, busking.

As well-seasoned a performer as you might be, busking takes a different set of skills and tests a different set of nerves in comparison to stage performance. It is one thing to play a venue where you have been contracted to appear (that alone offers more security and confidence than you may realize). It's quite another matter finding a spot in the middle of a busy pedestrian thoroughfare where neither shoppers, nor storekeepers, nor police will object to your presence.

The first thing to understand about busking is that there are no steadfast rules. However, there are certain guidelines that, when followed, are likely to increase your tips, and others that will most assuredly keep you in good graces with fellow buskers—an angry juggler lobbing a flaming bowling pin into your tip basket is not a good thing.

Be Prepared

Before packing up and heading into the streets, go over the following checklist:

> **1. Appearance.** Anything goes, but being clean and groomed keeps you from being considered just another worthless beggar. Something with a bit of flair can help draw attention, too. Especially in more crowded or spacious locations, it can be difficult to hear or locate musicians. Make it easier for people to spot you.

> **2. Sheet music.** Leave it behind. Not only is it at the mercy of the faintest breeze, it also creates a barrier between you and the audience. Memorize a minimum of 20–30 minutes of material, and keep your head up and your eyes on the passersby. This goes for group performers as well; I've seen countless string quartets perform at London's Covent Garden without stands and sheet music. In fact, they prance and spin and stomp through the likes of "Eine Kleine Nachtmusik" and Radetzsky's "March" and are immensely popular with the crowd.

3. Repertoire. As lovely as they might be, airs, largos, and other slow-paced works just don't cut it, regardless of how passionate and resonant they might be. Bright, toe-tapping tunes are the best crowd pleasers. Put snobbishness aside, cut out the schmaltzy, pedantic bits, and stick to classic music excerpts, if you must. Tunes from popular songs and folk-dance music work well. Celtic pieces—reels, jigs, polkas, and quick-paced hornpipes—are my personal favorite.

4. Tip catcher. Have something—your case, a large hat, a box, or a basket—into which people can throw tips. And they do throw, so make it something with a wide opening; some folks like to drop their offerings without ever slowing their pace. Choose something reasonably easy to see and not easily tipped over (dazed pedestrians routinely stumble over even my royal-blue-lined fiddle case). Depending on the venue you choose, you might even hire a charming friend or a winsome older child or teen to pass a jar or basket through the crowd.

5. Seed money. Don't leave home without it! This is one of those unexplained mysteries of the universe—an empty tip basket takes longer to fill than one that has been "seeded." Moreover, if you want to grow dollar bills, don't plant copper pennies. Generally, a single dollar bill and a couple of quarters will suffice. In other countries (did I mention that busking is an excellent means of supplementing your travel funds?), you will probably want to stick to the higher-denomination coins.

Location, Location, Location

Once you are prepared and ready for your performance, you'll want to head for areas heavily trafficked by pedestrians who are not in a hurry to get anywhere (by contrast, sports fans en route to a game are not likely to register you as anything other than a bothersome obstacle). Outdoor pedestrian shopping malls are great, as are old town centers with narrow streets traveled by shoppers and tourists, wide sidewalks near tourist attractions, and museums.

Even better is to locate yourself near some place where people have cause to loiter—outdoor cafés and markets or snack-bar kiosks, even bus and metro stations where people have reason to pause and reach into their pockets anyway. Public parks and city squares with fountains and benches where people go to socialize and relax are also good. The timing can be critical, but will vary according to location. Generally, late morning or early afternoon is the soonest you'll want to venture out. Early evening, 4:30 or 5 p.m., is often a good time as well. You will have to determine this for yourself.

Photo by Joshua Berger

Cellist Sean Grissom entertains at one of the coveted spots in the New York subway system.

MAKING YOUR LIVING AS A STRING PLAYER

After finding a populated area, scout around for a spot that will work to your best advantage. Don't look too long, as other buskers can slip in quickly and take the best spots, but take enough time to ensure that you are not intruding upon another performer's space, physical or sonic. You might even choose to wander the fringes of outdoor cafés or hop on subways (although the legality of this is dubious) with a hanging tip basket or with a partner to collect tips for you. I prefer to remain stationary, though. When possible, set up near a wall or in an unused alcove, usually a closed shop front, that will project your sound outward. Don't hide in the back, however; put yourself out toward the front where folks can see you.

Narrow, winding pedestrian streets have the same acoustical effect, but try to find an intersection so as to reach a larger audience. Underground subway passages also have good acoustics and sizeable crowds, but it is not always legal to perform in them. In London, daring buskers routinely ignore posted signs threatening penalties of up to $300.

Often, you will not have the luxury of optimal acoustics. In this case, I usually try for a lamppost, a tree, or a fountain to put my back to—something stationary that forces the crowd to part. Strange as it seems, unless you have a sound system or play bagpipes, people will manage to stumble over your tips, if not you. A storefront—or rather, the space between stores—works well. Avoid crowding close to entryways (customers feel panhandled) and blocking window displays.

Fair Play

Some cities require permits for street performance, although I've not yet seen it enforced anywhere. It's best to ask the local police or chamber of commerce about any restrictions—although unless signs are posted, you'll most likely just be asked to move on. In London's Covent Garden, I was just nearing the end of my first reel when a policeman gently tapped me on the shoulder. In typical British fashion, he politely asked that I not perform on what he explained was privately owned sidewalk. Then, with a smile, he pointed to the other side of the building.

"I think if you move down toward the station, you'll find the tips much better there, anyway."

In Dusseldorf, Germany, a territorial shoe salesman waited exactly 30 minutes before confronting me with emphatic tones and waving hands, which clearly stated that I should clear out. Although I doubted his right to do so, I acquiesced, rather than cause a scene.

Some places requiring permits do have rules about changing locations every 30 minutes, or have a grid system, which will be explained to you. In unregulated towns, you may occasionally find that you have inadvertently set up in some regular's spot. On the other hand, sometimes fellow performers, particularly bands, will be single minded and hardly notice your presence. It is best to pack up and leave of your own accord, dignity intact, rather than have them blast you away. Others will loiter, usually waiting for a break in your routine to inquire how much longer you will be. Be gracious and accommodating; they might prove to be useful connections. Sometimes if you are friendly and professional and their performance is more visual than audible (mimes, balloon artists), they might offer to share space. This arrangement often works to the benefit of both: people who wouldn't slow down for music will stop to watch the antics of a juggler and wind up enjoying—and tipping—both of you.

A quick word on using amplifiers: if you choose to go this route, have a heart and show a little courtesy towards fellow performers. There are plenty of fans and tips out there for all of us. There is no need to crank the volume so loud that you clear the area of other buskers for blocks around.

Safety First

Once you have found your spot, place your case or tip basket (with seed money!) approximately two to three feet in front of you, if the pedestrian traffic permits. Generally, people like to maintain a "safe" distance, preferring not to get too close.

While I have neither experienced nor heard tell of any foul play while busking, I am always watchful. If I set my fiddle down, I hover over it; if I stop to talk to someone, I move closer to my tips, remaining alert. I keep my belongings in front of me, within leg's reach. Though I have never felt myself or my instrument to be endangered, I have been wary of the interest that some passersby (usually beggars) have taken in my tips. In that event, I keep an eye out, ready to kick my case closed over my tips if I see them again or if they venture too close.

When I've finished, I pause a bit, loosening my bow, preparing my fiddle for storage, giving listeners the opportunity to realize that the show is over. Usually at least one or two people surprise me with a last-minute tip and compliment. Then I scoop my earnings into a bag—never stopping to calculate the take—tuck it quickly away, and disappear.

Powerful Performing

When you perform, stand up, if your instrument allows. It makes you more visible, and you appear more energetic, which appeals to an audience. I find it helps to be passionate about performing. Dance and sway to the music, enjoy yourself. Pour energy into the crowd, and it will generally be returned—both in smiles and tips. In Madrid, after nearly 15 minutes of performing with timid uncertainty and travel-weary fatigue, I received little more than scorn from the high-class matrons and indifference from the rest. I did a quick attitude adjustment and decided to kick back and just enjoy myself, despite the fact that I needed the money.

Within minutes, the tides turned. Faces lit up with delighted smiles, photos were snapped, tips were tossed along with words of praise. There is something to the old adage "As ye sow, so shall ye reap."

As a solo performer, particularly if you are not using an amplifier, you are not likely to draw a crowd. This is no reflection on your talent, just a matter of comfort or even culture. In many countries, people seem slightly intimidated by soloists. In a group, the attention is dispersed, making it safer to stop, enjoy, and move on, often without tipping. If it is just you and them, however, there is a sense of guilt for "taking" your music without leaving something in return, so listeners tend to keep their distance. They will loiter before window displays, lean against trees while waiting for their spouses, rest on nearby benches—but you can spot them. Their feet will be tapping; they may even permit a smile to grace their lips. Some might even jig a step or two as they pass. Children will turn their heads and clap their hands. They may not tip, but they are enjoying what you offer, and they are, after all, your audience.

Accept it, laugh about it, relax, and have fun.

A few years ago, at the age of 74, I decided to assay the role of impresario and try to establish a new chamber-music series, to be played in the home. It turned out to be ridiculously easy.

—Edgar Bottler

Specialty of the House

7

How to start your own CHAMBER-MUSIC SERIES

By Edgar Bottler

MORE THAN 40 YEARS AGO, when I was a young lawyer, I had my second date with the young principal cellist of the Houston Symphony, the beautiful and talented Marion Davies. After dinner, she asked me if I would like to hear a little chamber music. I, of course, said yes. We went to pianist Albert Hirsh's house, where I was surprised to find her friend Isaac Stern warming up on his del Gesù violin and the irrepressible Gaetano Molieri tuning his viola. The rest of the evening consisted of Brahms' piano quartets being played to a fascinated audience of two.

It was my first experience of chamber music in the home—where it was meant to be played. I was hooked. For many years after that, I heard chamber music performed by wonderful musicians in my home and the homes of others. I was thoroughly spoiled.

When I moved to Seattle 16 years ago, I missed those house concerts, although I met many musicians and supporters of classical music in my roles as president of the Santa Fe Chamber Music Festival in Seattle and of the Seattle Symphony. So a few years ago, at the age of 74, I decided to assay the role of impresario and try to establish a new chamber-music series, to be played in the home.

It turned out to be ridiculously easy. I called up Susan Gulkis, principal violist and frequent soloist with the symphony, to find out how much money it would take to put on a concert. She told me it depended on how much music would be played and the time required for necessary rehearsals.

A light dawned. I knew from long experience with musicians that they like to play a run-through of their program with a small audience before performing it in a formal concert in a public venue. I decided to offer them the chance for a run-through with pay in a beautiful home. This would require no extra rehearsal time (thus saving me money) and would give them the opportunity to meet and talk with a sophisticated chamber-music audience.

I then talked with several past presidents of the Santa Fe festival, with chamber-music aficionados, with the symphony's music director, Gerard Schwartz, and with the influential music critic Richard Campbell. Everyone was wildly enthusiastic, especially since there would be no fund-raising, no paid staff, no 501(c)3 non-profit corporation requiring costly accounting— and I was going to do practically all the work. By this time I was confident that I could find suitable homes. I decided to make it simple: I would charge $100 for a membership, limit the number of members to 50, and put on four concerts a year. This would enable me to pay the musicians a flat fee of $1,000 per concert and leave some extra money for incidental expenses.

Campbell said I needed a name for the series, so I came up with "Dress Rehearsal," simple and descriptive. The only difficult choice was whether to start by signing up the members or contracting with the players. I decided to begin with the musicians, so I could present a formal schedule with outstanding chamber-music groups and players to potential members. I would have to underwrite any losses, but I was convinced that they would be small or nonexistent. At the suggestion of my accountant, I formed a simple nonprofit association and opened a bank account for it.

Everything went like clockwork. Every musical group I contacted wanted to play in the series. I signed contracts and then, with the help of two friends, assembled a list of prospective members. It required two mailings, but I reached the goal of 50. Then I contacted owners of beautiful homes who might be interested in participating. The issue of refreshments came up; we decided to limit them to sparkling water and white wine. (I happen to prefer red, but it doesn't look so fine when spilled on homeowners' carpets.)

So far, the concerts have been very successful. For the first, the Seattle-based Bridge Ensemble played piano quartets in a lovely house overlooking Lake Washington and the Olympic Mountains. The program included the world premiere of a quartet by noted Russian composer Giya Kancheli. This work had been commissioned by the Bridge for their first concert in Seattle's new Benaroya Hall. The second concert featured cellist Nathanial Rosen, who was in town to play concerts sponsored by the Northwest Chamber Orchestra, and pianist Adam Stern. They played Bach and Stravinsky in a contemporary home designed to display the owners' wonderful art collection. Rosen explained the various movements of each piece to a rapt audience.

Our third concert was held in our own home, with Susan Gulkis and friends playing works for violin, viola, and bass. The fourth concert featured internationally known violinist Ingrid Matthews and keyboard artist Byron Schenkman. They played early music in a wonderful old home overlooking Seattle and Elliot Bay.

We ended up with a cash surplus and decided to offer a $500 prize and recital to an outstanding music student at the University of Washington. Robin McCabe, director of the School of Music, chose violinist Jonathan Aldrich, who gave a wonderful recital in a fifth concert held in our home, which was well received by our audience. We have decided to make the award of this Director's Prize a regular part of each season.

The reaction of both musicians and our members to this chamber-music "experiment" has been very positive. I believe it would be very easy to duplicate this series in any city with experienced chamber-music players and an enthusiastic chamber-music audience. Anyone outside the Seattle area is welcome to use the name Dress Rehearsal, and I would be glad to send copies of my letters of invitation, notices of meetings, and letter agreements to any interested person.

Edgar Bottler can be contacted via e-mail at EDGARDOB@aol.com.

*Make your studio a nice place for kids;
sometimes children like to invite their
friends, and the enjoyment of observing
a music lesson can be a pivotal moment.*
                                    —John Blasquez

A Class Act

8

TIPS ON CREATING A HOME TEACHING STUDIO

By John Blasquez

SO YOU'VE DECIDED TO TEACH private music lessons. Congratulations! Comfortable as you are with your teaching skills, perhaps you're less certain about how to set up a home studio. Let's look at choosing a location, setting up a functional and comfortable studio, and co-existing harmoniously with your neighbors.

Location, location, location. Like property values, the success of a business often hinges on its location. Fortunately most people will go out of their way to see a reputable teacher, so it's not imperative that you set up shop in the high-rent district at the center of town. On the other hand, don't locate your studio a scenic 50 minutes from anywhere.

You'll find many options: your home, a space in a music studio, a cubicle in a music store, the parks and recreation center or civic arts department, a church room, or a space in an office building. Studios outside the home have some advantages. They often come with built-in advertising and a steady stream of referrals. If you want to maintain a limited teaching schedule, sharing a studio with cooperative people may be the perfect solution. There's also the benefit of meeting and networking with other teachers and musicians. And by starting off in a studio, you can try out teaching without turning your home upside-down, launching your career in an atmosphere that's more professional than the average family room.

However, many successful private instructors teach in their homes. Home studios tend to be comfortable and spacious, with a warm ambience that is hard to match in other settings, and they offer the most flexibility for setup and scheduling. Other advantages of the home studio include the short commute and a kitchen that's always open. Plus you can water the lawn, do your laundry, and download your e-mail between lessons. And if you use an entire room solely for business purposes, you may deduct it at tax time (as well as a percentage of your utility bills) as business expenses. If you're the home owner, just be aware that later you may have to recapture the depreciation.

Everyone has the right to operate a home-based business; however, your local planning department may require that you obtain a permit, and it may place certain constraints on business activities. Your rights and restrictions are usually spelled out in the Home Occupation section of the zoning ordinance. Fortunately, many ordinances include a clause that specifically endorses tutoring in the home. You may be able to find the home occupation statute online. Try searching for "home

occupation ordinance," "home occupation permit," or just "home occupation" or "home business." Include the name of your municipality. If you are in an unincorporated area, make sure that you're researching county ordinances.

Before You Start

Consider some of the following points when deciding how to set up a room in your house as a studio.

Parking. If possible, provide off-street parking. It's convenient for your students and courteous to your neighbors. Above all, consider the safety of the youngsters and do your best to keep them away from the street.

Bathroom access. Sometimes students just need to wash their hands. Then, of course, there are the calls of nature, and the kid who needs to switch into a soccer uniform after a lesson.

Space. Afford yourself a large open work area if possible, preferably about six by nine feet, with room enough to get to both sides of a student so you can observe from different vantage points. And leave enough room next to the student's seat for an extra armless chair or stool so that an interested parent can look on. In addition, you'll want to get up from your chair once in a while simply to move around a bit, so make sure it's easy to do so.

Waiting room. Invite your students inside. When it's 92° F outside, it may feel like 120° F in your student's car. If you do not have a suitable room adjoining the studio, ask that people show up no more than five minutes early and keep some extra folding chairs or stools at hand. (You never know when back-to-back students will be accompanied by an entourage that includes the entire family plus a friend.)

Outfitting and Arranging Your Studio

If necessary, start with a Spartan studio. Countless teachers have produced astonishing results using only a music stand and adequate lighting. Choose a sturdy music stand, such as an orchestra stand that can support a heavy binder without swaying or twisting. High-quality folding stands are also available.

Of course, you can expand beyond this basic setup by getting a second music stand so that you can play duets with your students, and setting up a handy accessory shelf that attaches to your stand for holding pencils, erasers, rosin, and so on. An excellent combination is a Konig Meyer 10065 folding music stand plus the Manhasset accessory shelf.

So that children's legs aren't left dangling, provide a stool about 10 to 12 inches tall and wide enough for both feet. And for your own comfort and health, find a good-quality armless office chair.

Make room for any instrument that you play, including accompaniment instruments. If you don't have room for an acoustic piano, look into the better keyboards that are available today; some have impressive qualities of sound and touch.

Keep certain essentials within arm's reach: an electronic tuner or tuning fork, a tape recorder (certain Technics and JVC models include microphone inputs), a microphone (preferably a stereo mic on a boom; good microphones include the Shure SM 57 or SM 58, the AKG C 1000 S, and Sony's ECM-MS907 stereo mic), a binder in which to chart your weekly schedule and your students' progress and assignments, a box of cassettes, a stack of your favorite CDs, a metronome, a large hand mirror (to show students things they can't easily see from their perspective), and a current list of your students' phone numbers. Here's an important item to keep out of reach: the telephone. When someone calls during a lesson, let your answering machine respond. Don't use your student's lesson time to take a call. Also include a clock for all to see, a bulletin board, and a lost-and-found box. For detailed suggestions regarding accessories, see www.SingingWood.com/Accessories.html.

More than ever, the computer is a musician's tool. You can use it to record and play digital audio, record CDs, and run such MIDI applications as music notation and theory lessons. And you can get inexpensive software that allows you to adjust the playback speed of regular CDs, so your students can play along with the great recordings, but at slower speeds. Choices include Slow Gold for WinTel PCs, and Transkriber, Amazing Slow Downer, or RetroCD for the Macintosh, each under $50. Some of these titles also allow you to transpose tracks to different keys, set up practice loops, and ease the process of learning music by ear. For the best fidelity, connect your computer's sound output to the auxiliary channel of your stereo, or connect it to multimedia speakers. Always locate speakers near head level. Don't place your computer setup or stereo system directly against a wall. Leave enough room so you can get behind it for maintenance, rewiring, and replacement, or put the whole system on wheels.

A large desk can be the centerpiece in your studio. If it's deep enough, you can stack your stereo equipment on it and still have ample useable desk space. Short on square feet? Build up. Or remove the sliding doors from a closet and move your desk inside. Also, you'll want file cabinets for your bookkeeping materials and sheet music, bookshelves for software and CDs, and possibly a photocopier.

If you have enough room, provide a sofa or love seat. On an end table or bookshelf, put out easy-to-read books on music, such as *Making Music for the Joy of It*, by Stephanie Judy. Make your studio a nice place for kids; sometimes children like to invite their friends, and the enjoyment of observing a music lesson can be a pivotal moment. So don't forget the comics and a small box of safe toys to occupy the wee siblings!

The Impact of Working at Home

And now a necessary word on the social realities of working at home. Your activities will affect family members and housemates on many fronts. Here's some of what your co-habitors can expect: increased phone calls, noise (i.e., music), parking problems, being awakened by an early morning lesson, kids making their way to the bathroom, more phone calls, the occasional car that's stuck in the mud until the tow truck arrives. And the biggest issue of all: if you use shared living space for your teaching, other household members will have to evacuate the area while you work. Count on regular surprises for the first few months; later you'll come to accept these as part of a normal workday.

Oh, and a separate phone line will go a long way toward keeping housemates happy.

Love Thy Neighbors

Now consider your neighbors. You'll probably find that they are overwhelmingly supportive of your career and good fortune. To them, you look like a living example of the American Dream— you're self employed, working at home, and contributing to society through a satisfying career. But even if you're the best possible neighbor and you run your business with the utmost consideration, you may encounter a person who feels compelled to complain. Handle this with diplomacy, for an inconvenienced, frightened, or angry neighbor can round up the posse quicker than you can say, "once again with feeling"— even when you're fully within your rights.

Likely neighborhood issues include noise, parking, traffic, security, and unfounded fears about where this is all going to lead. Bear in mind, it's easiest to solve neighborhood issues before they escalate. So get to know your neighbors. Say hello, lend a hand, offer to entertain at the block party, and donate a coupon for a free lesson or two to the neighborhood raffle. If your neighbors know you and trust that you'll respond reasonably and intelligently to their comments or requests, they're much more likely to voice any grievances or concerns.

Setting up your own studio can be one of the most satisfying moves in your career. So do your research, talk to your housemates and your neighbors, consider your own needs, and start off with the basics in equipment and studio space. And remember, teaching music is part music and part business. Attend to both and you may successfully launch and sustain a truly rewarding career.

The limited job prospects for today's music-school graduates have made working overseas a very attractive option to the freelance circuit—even if you're not wintering in Minneapolis.
—Jana Luckey

One of the best parts of living and working in central Europe is that it is the heart of Western classical music."
— Christopher Whiting

Have Passport, Will Play

9

AMERICAN STRING PLAYERS FIND OPPORTUNITIES AROUND THE WORLD

By Jana Luckey

IT WAS THE DEAD OF WINTER in Minneapolis. Temperatures were frigid, the snow was piled high. Roland Moyer's phone rang. It was an old friend of his, now with an orchestra in Porto, Portugal. He told Moyer about a principal bass opening in the Orquestra Metropolitana in Lisbon. Send them a tape, his friend urged. You'd love it here.

Moyer needed a change, fast. After serving for several years as principal bass of the Windsor Symphony in Windsor, Ontario, Moyer had moved out to Minnesota to be near friends, give up the pressures of orchestra playing, and start a teaching studio. He was doing office work, though, to make ends meet, and Portugal sounded like an awfully good idea.

By the time Moyer contacted the Lisbon orchestra in March of 1996, the administration was so anxious to fill the position that he was invited to come over right away to finish out the season. Armed with a single suitcase and his bass bow, Moyer flew to Portugal, less than a month after that fateful phone call.

"I stepped off the plane in Lisbon, still wearing my winter boots. It was 80 degrees! I hadn't slept in two days and I had to make a 10 a.m. rehearsal. When I got to the hall, everybody was speaking in 60 zillion languages. They gave me a bass to play, and I went to work."

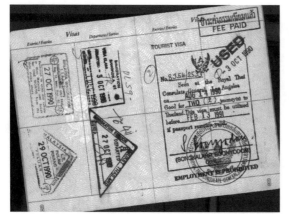

The limited job prospects for today's music-school graduates have made working overseas a very attractive option to the freelance circuit—even if you're not wintering in Minneapolis. Especially for those graduates seeking a full-time orchestra position, taking auditions for foreign orchestras broadens their options considerably. In 1989, Dona Nouné-Wiedmann was a graduate student in violin at Northwestern University who had been taking orchestra auditions for about two years.

"I was getting sick of it," she says. She was dating a German exchange student who was about to return home, and she "made a very spontaneous decision to give the German orchestras a try. At that time, they were still hiring lots of Americans."

Elizabeth Wooster, a harpist, auditioned successfully for the Singapore Symphony last summer, just after completing her master's degree at the Cleveland Institute of Music. She had decided that she wanted to pursue an orchestral career but was daunted by the low number of openings. "It's so difficult getting a job," she laments, "and I thought [the Singapore job] would be a good, practical experience. I hope it will put me in a position to get a better job in the States when I return."

Of course, Wooster may choose not to return—at least, not right away. Timothy Frank, a cellist with the Hong Kong Philharmonic, won the audition in 1995 when he was 24 and "feeling adventurous...I thought the job would be great experience. I didn't plan to stay over here for more than a couple of years, but things have unfolded in such a way that it feels worthwhile to stay here now." Frank's musical life in Hong Kong is rich and includes numerous activities outside of the orchestra.

Lands of Opportunities

Other musicians lucky enough to hold positions in North American orchestras look at opportunities overseas as a way to further their career goals. John Stokes, a Canadian cellist trained in the States, took a leave of absence from his associate-principal position with the Windsor Symphony in 1994 to study in Barcelona with Lluis Claret, a teacher he had met during a residency at the Banff Centre.

"Before coming overseas, I thought my career plans were generally to bounce around from orchestra to orchestra— hopefully about every five years—and eventually find a situation where the hassles of the job didn't overshadow the possibility of making music," Stokes says. "I've always had the idea that the [purpose of landing] an orchestra job was to create stability so I could do other creative musical projects on the side, such as quartets or contemporary music."

Job openings are limited in Canada, and the chances of winning another full-time position with a Canadian orchestra were extremely slim. Stokes enjoyed living in Europe so much

Cellist John Stokes goes sight-seeing on the Canary Islands.

that he applied to orchestras in Great Britain, Germany, and Spain. As luck would have it, when he was down to his last $3.50, he succeeded in winning a co-principal position with the Orquestra Sinfónica de Tenerife in the Canary Islands. He has since resigned from the Windsor Symphony and now earns approximately $27,000 to $29,000, which places him among the top 6 percent of wage earners in Spain.

The Audition Process

Americans find out about openings in orchestras overseas through a variety of means. It's common to see positions in foreign orchestras advertised in the monthly union journal *International Musician*. The music directors of both the Singapore Symphony and the Hong Kong Philharmonic often come to the States to hear live preliminary auditions. As a result, Americans make up 10 to 15 percent of both these orchestras.

The effort expended by these orchestras to audition Americans reflects their need for players of certain instruments. Openings for wind, brass, and lower string instruments are most frequent because, as Lan Shui, conductor of the Singapore Symphony, notes, "Piano and violin are the most popular instruments" throughout much of Asia.

Finding an orchestral position in Europe requires more initiative. When Nouné-Wiedmann decided to try to find a job in Germany, a friend helped her apply to a selection of German orchestras. Despite her strong résumé, which included experience playing with the Rochester Philharmonic Orchestra and other professional groups, the Nürnberger Symphoniker was the only orchestra that invited her to audition. John Stokes claims that he has applied to audition for 50 orchestras in Germany over the past three years and laughs, "I've been invited to audition three times for the same orchestra!" Nouné-Wiedmann and Stokes agree that since reunification in 1990, the influx of East Germans has created an oversupply of qualified musicians for the available positions.

Christopher Whiting, now a violinist with the Orchester der Oper Zürich, established contacts in Europe by participating in master classes in Zurich with Nathan Milstein and Lucerne with Franco Gulli while still a student at U.C. Berkeley. An invitation to be assistant concertmaster of the Festival Strings Lucerne, which arose from his appearance at the Gulli master class, proved to be a springboard to other opportunities in Switzerland.

The audition process in Europe has traditionally stressed the performance of solo works. Excerpts from the orchestral repertoire are often required for the audition, but as Nouné-Wiedmann suggests, "I really believe that it was my musicality that won the audition, and not my technical mastery of the excerpts." Stokes has seen principal chair audition lists that consist simply of the first movements of the Haydn D Major and Dvorák cello concertos and the principal cello solos from Richard Strauss's *Don Quixote*. Most commonly, however, string auditions in Europe require the first movements from both a classical and a Romantic concerto and a handful of orchestral excerpts.

Whiting has found that in Switzerland an audition is "less of a cattle call" than what he experienced in San Francisco. "Typically, there are between 10 and 20 candidates who play at an audition," he says. "This is because the orchestras audition every couple of months until a position is filled, and there are many more orchestras and available positions."

Nouné-Wiedmann's experience in Germany has been similar. By the time she was invited to audition for the Nürnberger Symphoniker, the orchestra had already held three auditions for the vacant tutti violin chair. The first audition had been restricted to Germans. "About 20 applicants are invited to our auditions, and they're selected based on the experience in their résumé. You don't want to be too experienced, though, because there's an age limit."

Stokes puts it more succinctly: "In Germany, if you don't have a professional position by age 30, forget it." Generally, older applicants are not invited to auditions unless they already hold a titled chair in one of the premier orchestras.

An aspect of German auditions that Nouné-Wiedmann has found unusual, she says, is that "Everyone in the orchestra is welcome to attend the auditions, and most of them do come." A simple majority vote of all those present, including the music director, sends players to the next round. While her audition for Nürnberg was not screened, Nouné-Wiedmann has found at auditions elsewhere in Germany that the use of a screen is becoming more common. This trend may be occuring for the same reason screens have become customary in the States— they eliminate ethnic or gender bias. As the borders between members of the European Union become more permeable and applicant pools become even more diverse, the possibility of discrimination becomes more of an issue.

At this point, Americans are a presence in orchestras around the world. The demand for full-time orchestra positions is so great on the part of today's music school graduates that most overseas orchestras do not need to actively recruit Americans. In the Orquestra Sinfónica de Tenerife, most of the 90 players are Spanish, though there are currently seven Americans and five Canadians. Stokes says that since he's been working there, the successful audition candidates have mostly been Russians and Americans. "Eastern bloc people are desperate to get out of their country," he explains, "and the North American job market forces musicians to look elsewhere for a career. To put it bluntly, North Americans and Eastern bloc people have sufficient fire under their asses to get a job in a foreign country, whatever the cost."

The Orchester der Oper Zürich does not specifically recruit Americans but, says Whiting, "They come in huge numbers anyway. The orchestra, and especially the immigration police, would prefer to hire Swiss musicians, but the demand for top-quality classical music far exceeds the country's ability to produce top-quality Swiss musicians." He calculates that foreign applicants for violin positions with his orchestra exceed by nearly tenfold the number of Swiss applicants. He believes it should be even easier to attract able American players now that he has convinced the orchestra to state the impressive salary (approximately $70,000 before taxes) in its audition announcements. As Whiting explains, "The Swiss don't talk about money. In some private companies, discussing one's salary is grounds for immediate dismissal."

Of course, it's one thing for Americans to take the auditions. It's quite another to win one. Clearly, orchestras worldwide find the American style of playing attractive. In Singapore, Lan Shui values versatility in the players he hires and often finds it in American candidates. "I think for orchestra playing, flexibility is very important. The orchestra has to be able to play in different styles and move between them easily."

Timothy Frank says that David Atherton, the British conductor of the Hong Kong Philharmonic, "admires the U.S. conservatory system" and will do an audition tour in the States when there is an opening in the orchestra specifically to attract American applicants.

"My conductor is Spanish, but he really values the American conservatory training," Stokes says. "You don't have to teach an American how to play Mozart differently from Stravinsky." Because they've been studying the orchestral literature, he adds, "they're better prepared for the job. And they have a strong work ethic."

Cultural Barriers

The drive to obtain a position is so strong among Americans seeking their first job—or a better one—that concerns about cultural and language barriers are hardly acknowledged. Nouné-Wiedmann didn't know any German when she won her position in Nürnberg: "Only *auf Wiedersehen* and *Gesundheit!*" During her first season, her greatest fears were realized when the conductor would ask the orchestra to start at measure number 157. Fortunately, she contends, "Music is music, and you can get by without understanding everything the conductor says, as long as you have a helpful stand partner."

Whiting has struggled to overcome the language barrier. "Switzerland is pretty complicated when it comes to languages. There's Swiss German, which has very little in common with the German spoken in Germany or written in the newspapers, French, Italian, and Romansch—a leftover from ancient Roman occupation. I stick to "high German" at work and in daily life. It took countless hours of struggle to get it to its current modest level. True integration into Zurich society would require speaking one of the more than 30 local dialects."

Whiting married a Swiss woman, which has accelerated his mastery of the language.

In his quest to improve his Spanish, Stokes concurs that relationships make a difference. "Having a girlfriend you can only speak to in Spanish helps!" he says. "My Spanish is better than many of the Americans [in the orchestra] because I just forced myself to talk to people in Spanish. I made a lot of mistakes and got laughed at, but I was corrected and I learned."

The Americans working in Singapore and Hong Kong actually experience far fewer language difficulties. "Children in Singapore are taught both English and Chinese," explains Wooster. "And all signage is in English."

Frank uses English in Hong Kong but has learned a vocabulary of place names in Cantonese for when he travels by taxi. As a result of the return of Hong Kong to Chinese sovereignty on July 1, 1997, more conductors from the mainland are guest-conducting the Hong Kong Symphony; most of them not only don't speak English, but are fluent only in Mandarin, the language of mainland China.

In rehearsal, Chinese members of the orchestra do their best to translate for the English speakers. And both Singapore and Hong Kong are such international cities that the lifestyle is quite westernized, although Wooster is preparing herself for the transition. "I know there's a law for everything, like no chewing gum or spitting on the street," she says.

Once Americans working abroad manage to conquer the language problem, they are still challenged by cultural differences. Moyer is an avid runner and had every intention of maintaining his fitness regimen while in Lisbon. He found, however, that while Olympic-caliber runners are considered national heroes in Portugal, joggers are met with critical and curious stares. Moyer kept running, although he notes, "The fumes from all those little cars were so strong that I felt I was doing a real disservice to my lungs!"

Whiting came up against a difference that had an impact on his working relationships. "There is," he says, "a very particular greeting ritual in Switzerland. One must greet each person by name, paying attention to who must be greeted formally and who informally. At the end of the day one must say goodbye, repeating the name. How this is done, and if it is done, has great significance. I have unwittingly insulted a couple of Swiss orchestra members through my lousy greeting technique. It's not the thought that counts, but [following] the procedure."

Nouné-Wiedmann, a Lebanese-American who had lived in Beirut, London, and several U.S. cities before going to work in Germany, still found it difficult to adapt to certain aspects of German culture. "It has taken me a long time to develop *Deutche ordnung*, the sense of order so typical of Germans," she says. "After the overture, we would go offstage so the stagehands could rearrange the stage for the concerto. I'd always forget to close my music folder, and this really annoyed the stagehands. This was a really serious transgression to them."

Her marriage to the German student she'd met back in Chicago has undoubtedly helped her to adjust to other aspects of life in Nürnberg.

The Lifestyle

Once they meet the challenges of integrating into the local culture, Americans working overseas find a lot to recommend it. Stokes found the lifestyle in Barcelona, where he studied before getting the job in Tenerife, extremely attractive. "You can work hard, but it's not your life," he says. "Get up, go to work, get an espresso and a croissant, take three or four hours for lunch . . . you have your little nap and go back [to work] for four hours and then come home for a late dinner." He decided to look for work in Europe because "Europe is so much more civilized. There is so much history, art, architecture...you meet intelligent, educated people who have some kind of world perspective and speak two to six languages."

Whiting also values the European outlook on culture. "One of the best parts of living and working in central Europe is that it is the heart of Western classical music. One feels this at practically every concert. The audience is informed and interested. There are many opportunities to play chamber music and perform as soloist, and with a little effort, an audience—and a nice fee!—can always be rummaged up. I have concert opportunities here that I wouldn't expect to have in California, such as orchestra tours in Asia, Europe, and South America."

Moyer agrees that the opportunities in orchestras overseas eclipse those offered by regional orchestras in North America. The Orquestra Metropolitana schedule provided an ideal mix of activities for many of his colleagues. Orchestra members worked three weeks out of every four, performing symphony concerts two weeks a month and solo or chamber music recitals during the third week. Musical opportunities outside the orchestra were frequent and high-profile, including, for Moyer, a performance of the "Trout" Quintet with pianist Maria João Pires and cellist Jian Wang.

Frank has found the musical life of Hong Kong stimulating, but he is also taking full advantage of the island lifestyle. "I have a speedboat that I own with a couple of buddies. We take it out and go around from island to island." He adds, dryly, "That's probably something I wouldn't be able to do as a musician back in the States."

For Nouné-Wiedmann, her job in Nürnberg provides benefits she could only dream of in the States. She went on leave from her position in 1995, when her first child was born. After the birth of twins in 2001, she was assured of a place in the orchestra upon her return.

Coming Home

Working overseas can provide answers to some important career questions for musicians. Most music-school graduates with degrees in performance consider their options to be teaching, orchestra work, chamber music, or some combination of the three. It is only through gaining experience in all those areas, though, that a professional musician can find a balance of activities that offers the greatest personal satisfaction.

Elizabeth Wooster expects to return to the States after fulfilling her two-year contract with the Singapore Symphony. For her, the position is an excellent first job and, at a salary of approximately $43,000, it pays well. The experience will undoubtedly help her determine whether she wants to spend the rest of her career in an orchestra setting. Timothy Frank finds that he can achieve a good balance of musical activities in Hong Kong while making an excellent living. In addition to playing with the orchestra, he teaches at a private international school and has started a string quartet on the side.

Moyer's experience in Portugal led him to the conclusion he was already close to reaching when he left the Windsor Symphony—that he doesn't want to be an orchestra player. Though the conductor of the Orquestra Metropolitana asked him to stay on for the following season, Moyer decided to return home. "I don't enjoy the pressures of being principal," he says. He now teaches 21 piano students and is happy to be off the stage and out of the limelight.

Marriage to Europeans has provided Dona Nouné-Wiedmann and Christopher Whiting with compelling personal reasons to remain in Europe. Their relationships have eased their transition to life in a foreign country and have removed some of the legal obstacles to working abroad long-term.

Whiting admits, "I get pretty homesick for San Francisco sometimes. But American orchestras have a reputation for being nearly impossible to crack; it would probably be an unreasonable risk to give up my job here."

Nouné-Wiedmann, who is 35, believes that her age will probably prevent her from being accepted to any more auditions in Germany. Even if she were to return to the States with her husband, she knows that American orchestras do not look much more kindly on older applicants. John Stokes echoes Nouné-Wiedmann's concern about returning home and facing an impossibly competitive job market. "At the moment, I am not considering moving back to North America because of the insane cost of doing an American audition and a one-in-100 chance of winning."

Besides, Stokes concedes, it's not a bad life in the Canary Islands. "There's sun all the time, mountains to climb, beaches to hang at, and the most insanely beautiful women on the planet. Life could be so good if I just stayed and bought a house and settled down…"

Don't believe him. Stokes's idealism remains intact, and his search is not yet over. He continues to take auditions in Europe, motivated by the same desire for a more fulfilling career that has led so many American musicians to venture abroad.

Programs that teach the would-be teachers are becoming more common. It makes sense, since many professional string players find that, for either economic or personal reasons, they are drawn to teaching.

—Sarah Freiberg

A good string-education major can just about pick his place in the country."

—Barbara Barber

Teaching the Teacher

10

OPPORTUNITIES FOR STRING PLAYERS WHO WANT TO BE PEDAGOGUES

By Sarah Freiberg

RECENTLY, I BUMPED INTO A FLUTE TEACHER at the local store, and I told her I was writing a piece about preparing musicians to teach. Her reaction, which I believe is a common one, was, "You can't learn to teach. It's something you do by instinct."

In fact, it often was true that musicians had to learn to teach by instinct, because there weren't many degree programs that addressed the subject. And it's still true that, for those who teach privately at the community or college level, players tend not to have much prior experience when they begin teaching private lessons. (However, if they plan to teach the Suzuki method or go into public schools, they must complete specific programs). I, for example, hold a doctorate in cello performance and have taught at both community music schools and universities. As a graduate student, I received invaluable experience in classroom teaching during a stint as a teaching assistant.

But, while I also taught cello students during that time, I never had formal training to do so. I learned by doing, and it wasn't always easy.

Now, however, programs that teach the would-be teachers are becoming more common. It makes sense, since many professional string players find that, for either economic or personal reasons, they are drawn to teaching. Lawrence Scripp, chair of the Music Education department at the New England Conservatory of Music, puts it this way: "When kids come to study, they want to be Pablo Casals. But there comes a point when they want to explain their own techniques to others. Teaching becomes learning, and learning becomes something they can do artistically."

Opinions vary as to whether today's degree programs actually provide performers with the information they need to teach effectively. Assistant professor of music Barbara Barber teaches violin and violin pedagogy at Texas Christian University, which offers undergraduate and graduate degrees in performance and Suzuki pedagogy. She feels that string teachers need more instruction than they have traditionally received. "Even in my department, there's [still] confusion about what pedagogy is," she says. "Pedagogy is the science of teaching: teaching how to teach.

"A lot of people don't realize how important it is. It's one thing to take lessons to improve your own playing skills, but it's quite another thing to teach a youngster."

Where to Begin

There are several ways that string players can go about learning how to teach, according to Barber. Music education degrees are for students who know they want to go into education, and who "love music and want to share it with children."

Students in these programs learn a little about all instruments but often receive no specific training on their own instruments. In fact, string-playing education majors may get less training on strings than non-string players. Performance majors, on the other hand, "just want to play—they don't think they will ever want to teach. If they're lucky, they may get one undergraduate survey course that skims the surface of the different pedagogical approaches."

When they get out into the world, they discover that teaching provides good flexible income, but they haven't had teacher training—even if they "have a knack for teaching," as Barber says. Students who know they want to teach search out undergraduate pedagogy programs, but these can be hard to find. No matter what you majored in as an undergrad, Barber recommends pursuing a pedagogy degree in a graduate program. "Advanced degrees complement either education or performance degrees and allow students to be really well equipped to teach in any number of settings," she says.

Barber also points out that there are additional ways to augment teaching skills, particularly for the established teacher interested in more training: retreats, conferences, workshops, and seminars on pedagogy, which are often offered by various associations during the summer. For example, the Suzuki Association of America offers its teacher-development program at many college campuses each summer. Most Suzuki teachers take advantage of these summer institutes.

"It stimulates your own playing to take pedagogy courses," Barber points out. "You can examine your own technique and break down your own playing into small steps."

(The SAA office provides information about these courses and can be reached at (888) 378-9854 or www.suzukiassociation.org.)

Basic Training

The Longy School of Music in Cambridge, Massachusetts, is one institution that has realized the need for pedagogical training for performers. Violinist Clayton Hoener is the associate chair of strings at Longy, which is unique in that it is small and, says Hoener, "has always had a flavor of intimacy within the realms of the school—there are no barriers between departments."

In fact, the school offers classes for toddlers (starting at age one), preparatory students, and amateurs, and also provides undergraduate, master's, and artist diploma degree programs. And at Longy, all string students pursuing performance degrees must take a year of string-teacher training. This two-semester course includes both academic study and hands-on teaching experience.

Besides performance degrees, Longy has also developed an M.M. in instrumental performance with a special emphasis in string pedagogy. As Hoener says, "I don't think that the role of schools [in the past] has been training for the outside world. We're beginning to see more and more now, with courses offered in such topics as the business of music. And we're going to see more and more string pedagogy."

The students who enroll in this program are probably going to combine performance with studio teaching. While they are not preparing to teach in public schools, they may be involved with after-school programs, and they will be well equipped to teach students of all levels. They take two years of teacher training, history of pedagogy, and independent study in a pedagogical topic of their choice. Hoener feels that this training really prepares them well.

"Teaching by example is a wonderful beginning," he says. "Aren't we trying to make the best performer *and* teacher? Isn't it more comforting to have teachers who have learned their trade before they hang up their shingles?"

That sentiment is echoed at the Eastman School of Music in Rochester, New York. It offers undergraduate degrees in education, as well as M.M. and M.A. degrees that include teacher certification. Many undergraduates double major in performance and music education and, if they finish their course work in eight semesters, return for a final semester of student teaching. Louis Bergonzi, past president of the American String Teachers Association, is a professor of music education at Eastman. Bergonzi feels that it is of utmost importance that music-education majors and performance majors value each other's work, so he has designed an outreach program that offers string lessons to third graders in Rochester public schools. String-education majors help faculty provide group lessons, while pedagogy majors give private lessons. The two groups observe each other.

Says Bergonzi, "They're teaching the same students, and they rally around each other."

This is important for fostering rapport between future public-school and private string educators. Bergonzi likens the types of instruction to a rain forest, commenting, "as long as everything is in balance, the plants all thrive—but if the balance shifts, things start to decay."

Building Community

He also mentions the availability of summer study for private teachers. "Private teaching can be isolating, so sharing with other seasoned teachers at workshops allows private instructors to become part of a larger community and connect with each other. It's healthy."

Bergonzi feels that there is education out there for students preparing to be teachers, if they know where to look. "When I interview high-school seniors who are looking at a variety of schools," he explains, "I tell them to ask two questions at their interviews: 'What are the performance requirements for music education majors?' 'Who in the music-education department does the string training?' The answers will demonstrate whether the school has a commitment to strings, and to developing the best teachers."

Like Barber, Bergonzi believes that master's programs are a terrific resource for would-be string teachers—and that now is a great time to be a graduate student in music education. When he began teaching at Eastman, Bergonzi wouldn't accept doctoral students, due to a lack of jobs available at graduation. "Now, however, many colleges realize the importance of music-education specialists and, as they develop new programs, they are providing an abundance of new jobs [in this field]. The doctoral students I have now at Eastman have already had job offers, and they are far from finishing their degrees."

The New England Conservatory of Music's Lawrence Scripp also believes that there's a strong need for music-education specialists. He's helping to develop a new approach to learning through music with Music-in-Education, which has a three-year grant from the U.S. Department of Education.

"Eighty percent of our graduates teach, but only five percent took music-education courses," he points out. "We're hoping this new program will change that."

The program allows NEC performance majors to obtain significant teaching experience as part of a Music-in-Education concentration. Conservatory students participate in different types of internships—from private teaching to artist-in-residence programs to coaching ensembles. Recently, for example, students introduced Dvorák to an American history class at the Boston Latin School. Not only is NEC developing partnerships with public schools in the Boston area, but it is also creating a charter school, where music will be an integral part of the educational program.

NEC aims to prepare its students to become artists, teachers, and scholars. Scripp hopes that conservatory students will realize the benefits that teaching brings to their own artistic development. The idea is to train students to take advantage of their own talents. "It's not just about teaching, it's about how to notice how to fit in, to become a resource," he says. "Music is not just performance, it's creativity, learning, a form of inquiry, a form of reflection. The point is not to water down artistic standards. We're not substituting teaching for learning music well."

Scripp feels that Americans support music, but not at the public-school level. "Parents with resources realize the importance of music, and community music schools are thriving. The demand for music teachers is very high," he claims. ASTA's Bergonzi agrees. In fact, Bergonzi says that the number-one problem in ASTA is keeping up with available jobs. "It is true that there is a lack of teachers," he says, referring to the widespread concern over dwindling music programs in public schools. But it seems clear that many students are learning privately.

"Look at the figures. According to the National Association of Music Merchants, stringed-instrument sales have increased 12 percent per year for each of the last seven years."

Speaking to these articulate educators, all of whom are passionate about teaching, made me optimistic about the state of string teaching in the United States today. A growing number of excellent programs are preparing future string teachers for the next century. The educators didn't always agree, but the sense I got from them is that public schools—particularly those in cities—lack both funding and good music programs. However, the interest in music is picking up, often at the community level, and there lies the current demand for skilled string teachers.

As Barbara Barber puts it, "A good string-education major can just about pick his place in the country. There are pockets of excellent string programs, but to have good school orchestra programs means that there must be private study available. You have to provide the right environment."

With innovative programs like the ones described here, universities and conservatories are trying to address this problem—while also providing their students with invaluable training.

All in all, this is a great time to be a string teacher.

About the Contributors

John Blasquez is a seasoned, award-winning performer. He has been a top finalist on four occasions at the National Old-Time Fiddler's Contest and has performed with many San Francisco Bay Area bluegrass bands. He has been a dedicated music instructor for the last 24 years. In his Walnut Creek, California, studio he teaches classical violin and fiddling, including bluegrass, Celtic, old-time, and Texas styles. He specializes in accelerated learning, memorization techniques, improvisation, and how to learn music by ear. He also teaches guitar and mandolin.

Edgar Bottler has served as principal cellist of the Houston Symphony and as president of the Santa Fe Chamber Music Festival in Seattle and of the Seattle Symphony.

Robert L. Doerschuk is a former editor of *Musician* magazine. For 17 years he worked at *Keyboard* magazine, where he won two ASCAP Deems Taylor Awards while moonlighting as a pianist in the San Francisco Bay Area. In February 2002, his second book, *88: The Giants of Jazz Piano*, was published by Backbeat Books. He now lives in Nashville, where some of his best friends are string players.

Sarah Freiberg, a Boston-based cellist and corresponding editor, is a member of the Handel and Haydn Society, Boston Baroque, and the Freeman/Freiberg Duo, and a founding member of the prize-winning Sierra String Quartet. She has edited two publications of Guerini cello sonatas, and her recording of them is available on Centaur. She teaches in the early music program at Boston University and the Powers Music School.

Tom Heimberg is a violist in the San Francisco Opera Orchestra and a former member of the San Francisco Symphony. He has also served as orchestra manager for the Opera. His music studies included two years in Paris as a Fulbright Scholar and Teaching Fellow, and he later did studies in the psychology of practice. For more than two decades he has taught the Art of Practice as an extension class at the San Francisco Conservatory of Music. He's currently on the board of directors of the San Francisco Performing Arts Library and Museum, and Local 6 of the American Federation of Musicians.

Jana Luckey has served as associate principal cellist of the Toledo Symphony and frequently performs in Michigan as a freelancer and chamber musician.

Heidi Montgomery, having all but abandoned her classical background, is primarily a Celtic fiddler. She performed as a stage and street musician for 12 years with the Colorado Renaissance Festival and at various venues around the United States. Since the fall of 1999, Heidi has been backpacking throughout Europe, collecting folk tunes and busking to pay her way. Writing is another means by which she hopes to support her travelling addiction.

Van Vinikow, a violinist, holds a Bachelor of Arts in Music from University of Oregon. Since 1976 he has lived in Reno, Nevada, where he studied with Philip Ruder at the University of Nevada. He founded his quartet, the String Beings, in 1982. Van has played at Harrah's Tahoe and Reno, backed up such singers as Frank Sinatra, Sammy Davis, Jr., and Dean Martin, and has performed with the Reno Philharmonic and Nevada Opera. His version of "We're in the Money" is featured on Minnesota Public Radio's *Marketplace*, on "up" days, during the Wall Street wrap up. ("I shrewdly inserted the sound of a slot machine pouring out coins in the intro!" he admits.)

Hal Leonard Proudly Presents Reference Books from

S T R I N G   L E T T E R   P U B L I S H I N G

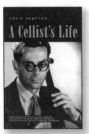

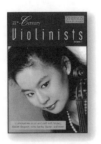
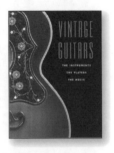
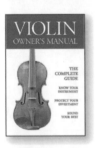

A CELLIST'S LIFE
Strings Backstage Series
_____00330753 (128 pages, 6" x 9")............$12.95

CUSTOM GUITARS
A COMPLETE GUIDE TO CONTEMPORARY
HANDCRAFTED GUITARS
_____00330564 (150 pages, 9" x 12")..........$39.95

ROCK TROUBADOURS
by Jeffrey Pepper Rodgers
Acoustic Guitar Backstage Series
_____00330752 (128 pages, 6" x 9")............$14.95

21ST-CENTURY CELLISTS
Strings Backstage Series
_____00330754 (128 pages, 6" x 9")............$14.95

21ST CENTURY STRING QUARTETS, VOL.1
Strings Backstage Series
_____00330530 (128 pages, 6" x 9")............$12.95

21ST CENTURY VIOLINISTS, VOLUME 1
Strings Backstage Series
_____00699221 (128 pages, 6" x 9")............$12.95

VINTAGE GUITARS
THE INSTRUMENTS, THE PLAYERS, AND THE MUSIC
_____00330780 (162 pages, 9" x 12")..........$39.95

VIOLIN OWNER'S MANUAL
_____00330762 (152 pages, 6" x 9")............$14.95

VIOLIN VIRTUOSOS
Strings Backstage Series
_____00330566 (128 pages, 6" x 9") $12.95

Prices, contents, and availability
subject to change without notice.

FOR MORE INFORMATION, SEE YOUR LOCAL MUSIC DEALER,
OR WRITE TO:

HAL•LEONARD®
C O R P O R A T I O N
7777 W. BLUEMOUND RD. P.O. BOX 13819 MILWAUKEE, WI 53213

Visit Hal Leonard Online at **www.halleonard.com**